THE
CRITICAL INFORMATION
WORKBOOK

CREATING A ROAD MAP
for your family™

AMY PRASKAC

On the Record Advance Planning™

Woodmere Press
Copyright © 2013 Amy Praskac
All rights reserved.
ISBN: 098896340x
EAN 13: 9780988963405

Table of Contents

Introduction: Completing Your Workbook

Congratulations on your commitment to organizing your critical information! You are going to create a road map for your family to follow in case of an emergency.

The ten sections in your critical information workbook are:
- Personal Information
- Personal Contacts
- Medical Information
- Last Rituals
- Legal Information
- Financial Information
- Personal Property
- Household Facts
- Document Locator
- Professional Contacts

The completed workbook will be a combination of information recorded directly in the workbook and directions about where to find information. For example, you will record information directly in the workbook about where you bank and the account numbers. You will note where you file your monthly statements—paper or electronic—and your annual tax returns.

Redundancy is built into the workbook. While much of the information is obvious to you, the purpose of the workbook is to compile this information for someone else to use. When you see information repeated in more than one section, this is to make it easier for someone who is not as familiar with your affairs as you are to find the needed information quickly.

Most sections have forms for each person; other sections have a form for the household. In the Financial Information section there are forms for two individuals, but if all of your financial accounts are jointly titled, you may choose to complete only one set of forms.

There are some important pieces of information that are *not* included in your critical information workbook. We *strongly* recommend that you store your social security number, passwords, and personal identification numbers in a *separate* location.

Some person or event likely prompted you to organize your records. Take a moment to write down your reasons. Return to your notes when you need motivation to complete the project. Use this Molly Haskell quote for inspiration if you need a starting point.

> *"But one of the attributes of love, like art, is to bring harmony and order out of chaos, to introduce meaning and affect where before there was none, to give rhythmic variations, highs and lows to a landscape that was previously flat." Molly Haskell*

My reasons for organizing my (family's) critical information are:

Tips for Completing Your Critical Information Workbook

- Commit to scheduling a regular time to work on your critical information workbook. You may use an electronic calendar or a paper calendar to schedule your time.
- Schedule working on your workbook to go with another related activity. For example, you may choose to work on your workbook after you pay your bills each month.
- Give yourself reminders and cues. You can program reminders in your paper or electronic calendar.
- Get an accountability buddy if you have trouble keeping commitments to yourself. Just knowing that someone will be asking about your progress can be a motivator.
- Reward yourself for progress.

Tips for Maintaining Your Critical Information Workbook

- Tell your family where you store your workbook.
- Make a back-up copy to store in another location: safe deposit box, executor, with a relative.
- Make changes in your workbook as they occur such as closing a bank account or changing an insurance policy.
- Schedule an annual review of your critical information workbook. Tie to another date such as an anniversary or when you file your income taxes when you will have been referencing your financial information.

On the Record Advance Planning

Personal Information

"It has long been an axiom of mine that the little things are definitely the most important."
Sherlock Holmes in *A Case of Identity* by Sir Arthur Conan Doyle

Background

The information in this section is typically what is required to complete a death certificate. You may want to wait until you complete the Last Rituals section before noting place of burial or disposition.

Get certified copies of any missing vital documents now. These are time consuming to replace. If you get them now, you will be prepared to provide them in an emergency.

Tasks

- ❑ Complete one Personal Information page for each person in your household.
- ❑ Get certified copies of any missing birth certificates and marriage certificates.
- ❑ Get copy of discharge papers (DD214) if missing.
- ❑ Rent a safe deposit box to store important and difficult to replace documents.

Resources

Where to Write for Vital Records
Centers for Disease Control and Prevention web site links to states and territories for users who want direct access to individual state and territory information. To use this valuable tool, you must first determine the state or area where the birth, death, marriage, or divorce occurred, then click on that state or area.
http://www.cdc.gov/nchs/w2w.htm

In many cases you can contact the county courthouse where the birth, death, marriage, or divorce occurred to get a certified copy of the needed document.

How to Request Military Service Records or Prove Military Service
National Archives and Records Administration web site has detailed instructions.
http://www.archives.gov/veterans/military-service-records/get-service-records.html

Bonus Idea

Start a conversation with your grandparents or anyone in your family interested in genealogy about the details of your family tree. You may hear stories that you have never heard before.

Full Name _____   *Person A*
                                                                 Include maiden name for women
Address _____   *who have taken their husband's*
                                                                 surname.
City _____ State _____ Zip _____

Telephones *Include area code.*

        Home _____

        Work _____

        Cell _____

E-mail addresses

        _____

        _____

Date of Birth _____ *MM-DD-YYYY*

Place of Birth *It is useful to know the county if you need to order birth certificates.*

City _____ State _____ Country _____ County _____

Father's full name _____   *Include maiden name for women*
                                                                     who have taken their husband's
Mother's full name _____   *surname.*

Spouse's full name _____

Date of Marriage _____ *MM-DD-YYYY*

Place of Marriage *It is useful to know the county if you need to order marriage certificates.*

City _____ County _____ State _____

Social Security Card _____ *location*

Your occupation _____ *former occupation if retired*

Place of burial or disposition_____   *Examples:*
                                                                       Fairview Cemetery in
_____   *Union City, New Jersey*
                                                                       Ashes to be scattered at sea.

If veteran, Service branch _____

Discharge papers filed _____ *location of Form DD 214*

Full Name _____ *Person B*
Include maiden name for women
Address _____ *who have taken their husband's*
surname.
City _____ State _____ Zip _____

Telephones *Include area code.*

      Home _____

      Work _____

      Cell _____

E-mail addresses

      _____

      _____

Date of Birth _____ *MM-DD-YYYY*

Place of Birth *It is useful to know the county if you need to order birth certificates.*

City _____ State _____ Country _____ County _____

Father's full name _____ *Include maiden name for women*
who have taken their husband's
Mother's full name _____ *surname.*

Spouse's full name _____

Date of Marriage _____ *MM-DD-YYYY*

Place of Marriage *It is useful to know the county if you need to order marriage certificates.*

City _____ County _____ State _____

Social Security Card _____ *location*

Your occupation _____ *former occupation if retired*

Place of burial or disposition_____ *Examples:*
Fairview Cemetery in
_____ *Union City, New Jersey*
Ashes to be scattered at sea.

If veteran, Service branch _____

Discharge papers filed _____ *location of Form DD 214*

Child's Name _____ *Child 1*

Date of Birth _____ *MM-DD-YYYY*

Place of Birth *It is useful to know the county if you need to order birth certificates.*

City _____ State _____ Country _____ County _____

Social Security Card _____ *location*

Name of School or Daycare 1 _____

Address _____

City _____ State _____ Zip _____

Contact Person _____Title _____

Telephone _____ *Include area code.*

Name of School or Daycare 2 _____

Address _____

City _____ State _____ Zip _____

Contact Person _____Title _____

Telephone _____ *Include area code.*

Medical Conditions and Allergies _____

_____

_____

Records & Prescriptions filed _____ *location*

Pediatrician _____ Telephone _____

Coach/Instructor 1 _____ Telephone _____

Coach/Instructor 2 _____ Telephone _____

Babysitter _____ Telephone _____

Emergency Contact _____ Telephone _____

Relationship to Child _____

Child's Name _____ *Child 2*

Date of Birth _____ *MM-DD-YYYY*

Place of Birth *It is useful to know the county if you need to order birth certificates.*

City _____ State _____ Country _____ County _____

Social Security Card _____ *location*

Name of School or Daycare 1_____

Address _____

City _____ State _____ Zip _____

Contact Person _____Title _____

Telephone _____ *Include area code.*

Name of School or Daycare 2 _____

Address _____

City _____ State _____ Zip _____

Contact Person _____Title _____

Telephone _____ *Include area code.*

Medical Conditions and Allergies _____

_____

_____

Records & Prescriptions filed _____ *location*

Pediatrician _____ Telephone _____

Coach/Instructor 1 _____ Telephone _____

Coach/Instructor 2 _____ Telephone _____

Babysitter _____ Telephone _____

Emergency Contact _____ Telephone _____

Relationship to Child _____

Personal Information

Child's Name _____ *Child 3*

Date of Birth _____ *MM-DD-YYYY*

Place of Birth *It is useful to know the county if you need to order birth certificates.*

City _____ State _____ Country _____ County _____

Social Security Card _____ *location*

Name of School or Daycare 1_____

Address _____

City _____ State _____ Zip _____

Contact Person _____Title _____

Telephone _____ *Include area code.*

Name of School or Daycare 2 _____

Address _____

City _____ State _____ Zip _____

Contact Person _____Title _____

Telephone _____ *Include area code.*

Medical Conditions and Allergies _____

_____

_____

Records & Prescriptions filed _____ *location*

Pediatrician _____ Telephone _____

Coach/Instructor 1 _____ Telephone _____

Coach/Instructor 2 _____ Telephone _____

Babysitter _____ Telephone _____

Emergency Contact _____ Telephone _____

Relationship to Child _____

Personal Contacts

"It's the friends you can call up at four a.m. that matter."
Marlene Dietrich

Background

Think of this list as a telephone tree. Include key people who will call other people in an emergency. Someone can use your address book if it is necessary to call everyone in your life.

There is a column to note the relationship in case someone who does not know your family and friends makes telephone calls on your behalf.

There is a column to note city and state (or country) so that the caller has some idea of the time zone.

Tasks

- ❑ Complete the list of Personal Contacts to be notified in an emergency.
- ❑ Update your address book. This can include adding new people or deleting people no longer in your life as well as correcting out-of-date information.

Bonus Idea

Get in touch with someone in your life that you have not talked or written to recently.

On the Record/Advance Planning™

Name	**Relationship**	**Telephone**	**City, ST**
Include first and last names.	*Examples: brother, cousin or friend*	*Include area code.*	*or country*
_____	_____	_____	_____
_____	_____	_____	_____
_____	_____	_____	_____
_____	_____	_____	_____
_____	_____	_____	_____
_____	_____	_____	_____
_____	_____	_____	_____
_____	_____	_____	_____
_____	_____	_____	_____
_____	_____	_____	_____
_____	_____	_____	_____
_____	_____	_____	_____
_____	_____	_____	_____
_____	_____	_____	_____
_____	_____	_____	_____
_____	_____	_____	_____
_____	_____	_____	_____
_____	_____	_____	_____
_____	_____	_____	_____
_____	_____	_____	_____
_____	_____	_____	_____
_____	_____	_____	_____
_____	_____	_____	_____
_____	_____	_____	_____
_____	_____	_____	_____

Address book filed _____ *Example: next to kitchen phone*

Think of this list as a phone tree for key contacts who must be notified immediately in an emergency. The city and state are included to give an indication of the time zone.

Medical Information

"Everything should be made as simple as possible, but not one bit simpler."
Albert Einstein (attributed)

Background

This is not intended to be a complete medical record, only a place to list key information needed in an emergency.

Tasks

❑ Complete Medical Information for each person.
❑ Review medical directives to make sure information is current.
❑ Discuss organ and/or body donation with your family.

Definitions

Advance Directive to Doctor and Family or Surrogates (Living Will)—allows you to express your wishes for care in the event that you cannot speak for yourself.

Directive Regarding Who May Receive Medical Information—is a form obtained from, completed, and filed with your health care provider.

Medical Power of Attorney—document designating an individual you name to make medical decisions on your behalf.

Out of Hospital Do Not Resuscitate Order (OOHDNR)—is typically completed only by persons under hospice care.

Bonus Ideas

Clean out your medicine cabinet. Get rid of out dated prescriptions and over the counter medications.

Transfer prescriptions so that all of your prescriptions are filled by one pharmacy. This is a safety measure.

Full Name _____ *Person A*

Medical conditions _____

_____

Medications _____

_____

_____

Allergies & Drug Reactions _____

_____

Append another page if you need more room or merely note where the list is filed. Examples: wallet, kitchen cupboard, or, if on the computer, enter the full file name.

Providers

Dentist _____

Address _____

City _____State_____ Zip_____

Telephone _____ *Include area code.*

Doctor _____

Address _____

City _____State_____ Zip_____

Telephone _____ *Include area code.*

Doctor _____

Address _____

City _____State_____ Zip_____

Telephone _____ *Include area code.*

Pharmacy _____

Address _____

City _____State_____ Zip_____

Telephone _____ *Include area code.*

On the Record Advance Planning

Medical Directives

Directive Regarding Who May Receive Medical Information

Date_____ *MM-DD-YYYY*

Original filed with_____ *health care provider*

Copy filed _____ *location*

Advance Directive to Doctor and Family or Surrogates (Living Will)

Date signed_____ *MM-DD-YYYY*

Original filed _____ *location*

Copy filed _____ *location*

Medical Power of Attorney

Date_____ *MM-DD-YYYY*

Person(s) Named_____

Original filed _____ *location*

Copy filed _____ *location*

Out of Hospital Do Not Resuscitate Order

Date signed_____ *MM-DD-YYYY*

Original filed _____ *location*

Copy filed _____ *location*

Organ Card or Body Donation Forms

Contact _____ *Organization /Institution*

Address _____ *Examples:*
Texas Organ Sharing All.

City _____State_____ Zip_____ *or Texas A&M Coll. Of Med.*

Web Site _____

Telephone _____ *Include area code.*

Card or Forms filed_____ *location*

Medical Insurance

Policy Number _____ Group Number _____

Company Name _____

Address _____

City _____ State _____ Zip _____

Web Site _____

Telephone _____ *Include area code*

Medicare

Claim Number _____

Effective Date Part A _____

Effective Date Part B _____

Medicare Choice Plan _____

Medicare Supplemental Insurance

Policy Number _____ Group Number _____

Company Name _____

Address _____

City _____ State _____ Zip _____

Web Site _____

Telephone _____ *Include area code.*

Take care with your Medicare card; it includes your Social Security Number. Losing your card may leave you vulnerable to identity theft.

Dental Insurance

Policy Number _____ Group Number _____

Company Name _____

Address _____

City _____ State _____ Zip _____

Web Site _____

Telephone _____ *Include area code*

Disability Insurance

Policy Number _____ Group Number _____

Company Name _____

Address _____

City _____ State _____ Zip _____

Web Site _____

Telephone _____ *Include area code*

Long Term Care Insurance

Policy Number _____ Group Number _____

Company Name _____

Address _____

City _____ State _____ Zip _____

Web Site _____

Telephone _____ *Include area code*

Vision Insurance

Policy Number _____ Group Number _____

Company Name _____

Address _____

City _____ State _____ Zip _____

Web Site _____

Telephone _____ *Include area code*

On the Record/ Advance Planning™

Prescription Drug Coverage

Policy Number _____ Group Number _____

Company Name _____

Address _____

City _____ State _____ Zip _____

Telephone _____

Web Site _____

Telephone _____ *Include area code*

Local Pharmacy

Name _____

Address _____

City _____ State _____ Zip _____

Telephone _____

Web Site _____

Telephone _____ *Include area code*

Mail-order Pharmacy

Name _____

Address _____

City _____ State _____ Zip _____

Telephone _____

Web Site _____

Telephone _____ *Include area code*

Full Name _____ *Person B*

Medical conditions _____

_____

Medications _____

_____

_____

Allergies & Drug Reactions _____

_____

Append another page if you need more room or merely note where the list is filed. Examples: wallet, kitchen cupboard, or, if on the computer, enter the full file name.

Providers

Dentist _____

Address _____

City _____State_____ Zip_____

Telephone _____ *Include area code.*

Doctor _____

Address _____

City _____State_____ Zip_____

Telephone _____ *Include area code.*

Doctor _____

Address _____

City _____State_____ Zip_____

Telephone _____ *Include area code.*

Pharmacy _____

Address _____

City _____State_____ Zip_____

Telephone _____ *Include area code.*

On the Record Advance Planning

Medical Directives

Directive Regarding Who May Receive Medical Information

Date_____ *MM-DD-YYYY*

Original filed with_____ *health care provider*

Copy filed _____ *location*

Advance Directive to Doctor and Family or Surrogates (Living Will)

Date signed_____ *MM-DD-YYYY*

Original filed _____ *location*

Copy filed _____ *location*

Medical Power of Attorney

Date_____ *MM-DD-YYYY*

Person(s) Named _____

Original filed _____ *location*

Copy filed _____ *location*

Out of Hospital Do Not Resuscitate Order

Date signed_____ *MM-DD-YYYY*

Original filed _____ *location*

Copy filed _____ *location*

Organ Card or Body Donation Forms

Contact _____ *Organization /Institution*

Address _____ *Examples:*
Texas Organ Sharing All.
City _____State_____ Zip_____ *or Texas A&M Coll. Of Med.*

Web Site _____

Telephone _____ *Include area code*

Card or Forms filed_____ *location*

On the Record Advance Planning

Medical Insurance

Policy Number _____ Group Number _____

Company Name _____

Address _____

City _____ State _____ Zip _____

Web Site _____

Telephone _____ *Include area code*

Medicare

Claim Number _____

Effective Date Part A _____

Effective Date Part B _____

Medicare Choice Plan _____

Medicare Supplemental Insurance

Policy Number _____ Group Number _____

Company Name _____

Address _____

City _____ State _____ Zip _____

Web Site _____

Telephone _____ *Include area code*

Take care with your Medicare card; it includes your Social Security Number. Losing your card may leave you vulnerable to identity theft.

Dental Insurance

Policy Number _____ Group Number _____

Company Name _____

Address _____

City _____ State _____ Zip _____

Web Site _____

Telephone _____ *Include area code*

Disability Insurance

Policy Number _____ Group Number _____

Company Name _____

Address _____

City _____ State _____ Zip _____

Web Site _____

Telephone _____ *Include area code*

Long Term Care Insurance

Policy Number _____ Group Number _____

Company Name _____

Address _____

City _____ State _____ Zip _____

Web Site _____

Telephone _____ *Include area code*

Vision Insurance

Policy Number _____ Group Number _____

Company Name _____

Address _____

City _____ State _____ Zip _____

Web Site _____

Telephone _____ *Include area code*

Prescription Drug Coverage

Policy Number _____ Group Number _____

Company Name _____

Address _____

City _____ State _____ Zip _____

Telephone _____

Web Site _____

Telephone _____ *Include area code*

Local Pharmacy

Name _____

Address _____

City _____ State _____ Zip _____

Telephone _____

Web Site _____

Telephone _____ *Include area code*

Mail-order Pharmacy

Name _____

Address _____

City _____ State _____ Zip _____

Telephone _____

Web Site _____

Telephone _____ *Include area code*

On the Record/Advance Planning

Last Rituals

"It is a fact that a man's dying is more the survivor's affair than his own."
Thomas Mann, *The Magic Mountain*

Background

Use the decision page as a basis for discussions with your family. If you choose to donate organs or your body, you *must* include your family in this decision as they will be asked for their consent at the time of death.

Tasks

- ☐ Discuss plans for last rituals with family.
- ☐ Complete Last Rituals forms for each person.
- ☐ Complete Place of burial or disposition in Personal Information section.

Resources

The Bucket List (2007) Written & Directed by Rob Reiner
With Jack Nicholson, Morgan Freeman, Sean Hayes, Rob Morrow

Lasting Images: Alternatives to Traditional Burial (2006) Documentary film by Hammond & Joan Hendrix

1,000 Places to See Before You Die: A Traveler's Life List (2003) by Patricia Schultz

Search online using the term "willed body" or "body donation" and the name of your state to find a medical school near you that accepts body donations. Be sure to have another plan in case this does not work out.

On the Record: Advance Planning

Search online using the term "organ donation" or "tissue donation" and the name of your state to find an association or organization that can provide information and forms for you to complete.

The Funeral Consumers Alliance is a nonprofit organization dedicated to protecting a consumer's right to choose a meaningful, dignified, affordable funeral.

Funeral Consumers Alliance

802-865-8300

For more information or to find an affiliate near you: *www.Funerals.org*

Bonus Idea

Write your obituary as a way to review your life accomplishments and set goals for things you still want to experience or accomplish.

Decisions for End-of-Life Planning for _____ *Person A*

This is a critical section of your workbook. Many people do not address these important decisions nor discuss their wishes with their family. Please take time to consider the questions below.

Checking the appropriate boxes, signing, and dating the page will give your family the basic information they need to carry out your last rituals. The questions on the succeeding pages concern only the details.

Discuss your decisions with your family to make sure that your family understands, agrees with your choices, and is ready to carry out your last wishes.

Organ, Tissue or Body Donation?   ☐ Yes ☐ No

Recycle medical devices: pacemakers, glasses, hearing aids?   ☐ Yes ☐ No

Visitation Gathering?   ☐ Yes ☐ No

Disposition of Remains?   ☐ Burial ☐ Cremation

Final Disposition of Remains?   ☐ Buried ☐ Interred ☐ Scattered

Arrangements?   ☐ Family-led at home ☐ Funeral Home_____

Service(s)?   ☐ Funeral ☐ Memorial ☐ Committal   *Name of Funeral Home*

    Instructions filed _____ *location*

Pre-paid Funeral or Funeral Insurance?   ☐ Yes ☐ No

    Documents filed _____ *location*

Pre-paid Cemetery Plots or Columbarium?   ☐ Yes ☐ No

    If yes, location of cemetery plot or columbarium _____

    Name of Cemetery or Facility _____

    City _____ State _____ Zip _____

    AND documents _____ location

Obituary?   ☐ Yes ☐ No

Arrangements

Organ, Tissue or Body Donation documents filed _____ *location*

Final Arrangements by _____ *funeral home*

Address _____

City _____ State _____ Zip _____

Telephone _____ *Include area code.*

If prepaid, documents filed _____ *location*

Visitation Gathering at _____

Address _____

City _____ State _____ Zip _____

Telephone _____ *Include area code.*

Funeral or Memorial Service at _____

Officiated by _____

Address _____

City _____ State _____ Zip _____

Telephone _____ *Include area code.*

Committal Service to be held at _____

Address _____

City _____ State _____ Zip _____

Information for Obituary *Also see Personal Information Section of workbook.*

Additional Information & Photograph filed_____ *location*

Charitable Donations to _____ *organization or institution*

Address _____

City _____ State _____ Zip _____

Telephone _____ Web site _____

Contact Name_____ Title _____

Instructions for Service

Music, including Hymns

Scriptures and/or Other Readings

Those to Be Invited to Speak

Pallbearers *Note active or honorary.*

Flowers

Other *Example: flag for veteran*

Decisions for End-of-Life Planning for _____ *Person B*

This is a critical section of your workbook. Many people do not address these important decisions nor discuss their wishes with their family. Please take time to consider the questions below.

Checking the appropriate boxes, signing, and dating the page will give your family the basic information they need to carry out your last rituals. The questions on the succeeding pages concern only the details.

Discuss your decisions with your family to make sure that your family understands, agrees with your choices, and is ready to carry out your last wishes.

Organ, Tissue or Body Donation?   ☐ Yes ☐ No

Recycle medical devices: pacemakers, glasses, hearing aids?   ☐ Yes ☐ No

Visitation Gathering?   ☐ Yes ☐ No

Disposition of Remains?   ☐ Burial ☐ Cremation

Final Disposition of Remains?   ☐ Buried ☐ Interred ☐ Scattered

Arrangements?   ☐ Family-led at home ☐ Funeral Home_____

Service(s)?   ☐ Funeral ☐ Memorial ☐ Committal   *Name of Funeral Home*

    Instructions filed _____ *location*

Pre-paid Funeral or Funeral Insurance?   ☐ Yes ☐ No

    Documents filed _____ *location*

Pre-paid Cemetery Plots or Columbarium?   ☐ Yes ☐ No

    If yes, location of cemetery plot or columbarium _____

    Name of Cemetery or Facility _____

    City _____ State _____ Zip _____

    AND documents _____ location

Obituary?   ☐ Yes ☐ No

Arrangements

Organ, Tissue or Body Donation documents filed _____ *location*

Final Arrangements by _____ *funeral home*

Address _____

City _____ State _____ Zip _____

Telephone _____ *Include area code.*

If prepaid, documents filed _____ *location*

Visitation Gathering at _____

Address _____

City _____ State _____ Zip _____

Telephone _____ *Include area code.*

Funeral or Memorial Service at _____

Officiated by _____

Address _____

City _____ State _____ Zip _____

Telephone _____ *Include area code.*

Committal Service to be held at _____

Address _____

City _____ State _____ Zip _____

Information for Obituary *Also see Personal Information Section of workbook.*

Additional Information & Photograph filed_____ *location*

Charitable Donations to _____ *organization or institution*

Address _____

City _____ State _____ Zip _____

Telephone _____ Web site _____

Contact Name_____ Title _____

Instructions for Service

Music, including Hymns

Scriptures and/or Other Readings

Those to Be Invited to Speak

Pallbearers *Note active or honorary.*

Flowers

Other *Example: flag for veteran*

Legal Information

"A well-ordered life is like climbing a tower; the view halfway up is better than the view from the base, and it steadily becomes finer as the horizon expands."
William Lyon Phelps

Background

While the section is just one page long, you may have much to do if you do not have a will and durable power of attorney or if you need to revise these documents.

Consider these factors when choosing an executor:

> *Closeness of the relationship.* You are asking this person to take on a big responsibility. Your executor should be someone close to you whom you trust. Also, realize that you will have no secrets from this person by the time they manage your estate and distribute your assets.
>
> *Ability of the person to do the job.* Choose a person who will act responsibly to carry out your wishes. Choose someone who will communicate with your heirs and treat them fairly.
>
> *Geography.* Managing an estate is easier if your executor lives in the same city that you do, although it can be managed from afar using electronic communications and express mail.

Tasks

- ❑ Review your will.
- ❑ Review your durable power of attorney.
- ❑ Review your trust, if you have one.
- ❑ Contact an attorney if you need to write/update your will, trust, and powers of attorney.
- ❑ Meet with your executor to review your affairs and his or her duties.

Definitions

Durable Power of Attorney—document that designates an individual named by you to carry out legal and financial transactions on your behalf.

Trust—an arrangement whereby one or more persons manage another individual's property and protect it for the benefit of others. An individual may control distribution of their property during their lifetime or after death. There are as many types of trusts as there are reasons for creating a trust.

Will—a legal document that directs how your estate is to be managed, names an individual to manage the estate, and provides for the distribution of assets among your beneficiaries. It may also name a guardian for minor children.

Resources

American Bar Association
321 N Clark St
Chicago, IL 60654
800-285-2221
Lawyer Locator:
abanet.org/lawyerlocator/searchlawyer.html

Learn about ethical wills at: *http://www.ethicalwill.com/index.html*

Who Gets Grandma's Yellow Pie Plate?
Order workbook, video, or educator's package from:
University of Minnesota Extension Service Distribution Center
405 Coffey Hall, 1420 Eckles Av
St. Paul, MN 55108
800-876-8636
http://shop.extension.umn.edu/SearchResults.aspx?KeyWords=grandma&searchType=Store

Bonus Ideas

Write an ethical will to pass your values on to future generations. See Resources.

You will add meaning to your gifts of personal items and family heirlooms if you tell why an item is meaningful to you and share stories about family members. More ideas in *Who Gets Grandma's Yellow Pie Plate?* See Resources.

Legal Information for _____ _Person A_

Date of Will _____ _MM-DD-YYYY for date signed_

Executor(s) _____ _Include area code._

Telephone _____ Telephone _____

Will filed _____ _location_

Copies filed _____ _location_

Date of Durable Power of Attorney _____ _MM-DD-YYYY for date signed_

Person(s) Named _____ _Include area code._

Telephone _____ Telephone _____

Durable Power of Attorney filed_____ _location_

Copies filed _____ _location_

Date of Trust _____ _MM-DD-YYYY for date signed_

Type of Trust _____ _Examples: Living Trust, Charitable Remainder Trust_

Trust Papers filed _____ _location_

Copies filed _____ _location_

Date of _____ _key document_ _____ _MM-DD-YYYY for date signed._

Filed _____ _location_

Copies filed _____ _location_

Date of _____ _key document_ _____ _MM-DD-YYYY for date signed._

Filed _____ _location_

Copies filed _____ _location_

Examples of key documents: citizenship papers, divorce decree or pre-nuptial agreement

Attorney _____

Address _____

City _____State_____ Zip_____

E-mail _____

Telephone _____ _Include area code._

Review your will periodically to make sure that it is current. Do an annual review with your executor and make sure that he or she knows where you file this workbook.

On the Record/ Advance Planning

Legal Information for _____ *Person B*

Date of Will _____ *MM-DD-YYYY for date signed*

Executor(s) _____ *Include area code.*

Telephone _____ Telephone _____

Will filed _____ *location*

Copies filed _____ *location*

Date of Durable Power of Attorney _____ *MM-DD-YYYY for date signed*

Person(s) Named _____ *Include area code.*

Telephone _____ Telephone _____

Durable Power of Attorney filed_____ *location*

Copies filed _____ *location*

Date of Trust _____ *MM-DD-YYYY for date signed*

Type of Trust _____ *Examples: Living Trust, Charitable Remainder Trust*

Trust Papers filed _____ *location*

Copies filed _____ *location*

Date of _____ *key document* _____ *MM-DD-YYYY for date signed.*

Filed _____ *location*

Copies filed _____ *location*

Date of _____ *key document* _____ *MM-DD-YYYY for date signed.*

Filed _____ *location*

Copies filed _____ *location*

Examples of key documents: citizenship papers, divorce decree or pre-nuptial agreement

Attorney _____

Address _____

City _____State_____ Zip_____

E-mail _____

Telephone _____ *Include area code.*

Review your will periodically to make sure that it is current. Do an annual review with your executor and make sure that he or she knows where you file this workbook.

Financial Information

"Money is better than poverty, if only for financial reasons."
Woody Allen

Background

You may not need all the forms in this section. You can record information on:
- Financial institutions
- Financial accounts
- Safe deposit box
- Credit cards
- Sources of income
- Debts
- Mortgages
- Life insurance policies
- Investment accounts
- Bonds
- Stock certificates
- Custodial accounts
- Retirement Accounts
- Pension accounts
- Qualified Domestic Relations Order (QDRO)
- Storage of financial documents

Be sure to note your safe deposit box number and the names of all signers on the safe deposit box. Always have at least two signers on your safe deposit box plus your executor. Keep documents that are difficult or expensive to replace in the box. If you will need the information on the documents, make a photocopy to keep at home.

Know how to contact the Human Resources Department at your place of employment for information about medical insurance under COBRA, life insurance, and income tax.

Tasks

- ❑ Complete Financial Information for each person. If you have joint accounts, you may need to complete only one set of forms. There are two sets of forms if you have separate accounts.
- ❑ Close inactive accounts.
- ❑ Order your free Credit Report.
- ❑ Verify that beneficiary forms for your life insurance policies are current or complete new beneficiary forms if yours are not up to date.
- ❑ Store pension papers, including QDRO, in safe deposit box.
- ❑ Turn any stock certificates over to a broker (ideal) or store in safe deposit box.
- ❑ Store bonds in safe deposit box. Keep a list of bonds at home.

On the Record Advance Planning

Definitions

Custodial account—created for the benefit of a minor at a financial institution and managed by an adult who is the custodian. Types of custodial accounts include: UGMA (Uniform Gift to Minors Act), UTMA (Uniform Transfer to Minors Act), Section 529, and Coverdell ESAs (Education Savings Accounts, sometimes referred to as the education IRA). These are tax-free ways to save for a child or grandchild's college education.

Pre-tax retirement accounts—IRA (Individual Retirement Account), Roth, 401(k), 403(b), Keogh, or SEP (Simplified Employee Pensions) for the self-employed.

Qualified Domestic Relations Order (QDRO)—a court order that recognized the right of the ex-spouse to receive all or part of a pension plan that belonged to their ex-spouse.

Resources

To get the free reports, you must go through this web site: *www.annualcreditreport.com.*

Go to Treasury Direct. at: *www.treasurydirect.gov/indiv/tools/tools.htm* for information on treasury bonds and notes, including tools to build an inventory and calculate what your bonds are worth today.

Bonus Ideas

Simplifying your finances can save time and money. If you have your checking, savings, certificates of deposit, credit cards at one institution, you may be able to get a consolidated statement. If you have a safe deposit box where you bank, you may get a discounted rate.

Check your credit report at least once a year to see if there is any unusual activity or errors. You are entitled to one free report a year from each of the credit agencies.

If you have more than six credit cards, you may want to consider which ones you use most frequently and close the other accounts.

Verify that your beneficiary forms are current. Check your account online or call the 800# for your retirement plan administrator. If you need to complete the forms again, follow these steps. Get the blank form. Make a copy of the blank form. Complete the form and sign it. Make a copy of the blank form. Complete the form and sign. Make a copy of the completed form. Keep the copy and the blank form in your files. Send the form with the original signature to the retirement plan administrator. The next time you need to change your beneficiaries, you will have a spare form on file.

If you hold stock certificates, consider filing the certificates with a broker who will maintain a "book record." Replacing and re-titling lost, destroyed, or inherited stock certificates can be an expensive and time-consuming process.

Roll over any 401(k) or 403(b) contributions you have left with a former employer's administrator to an account that you manage.

Banking

Financial Institution _____ *Person A*

Address _____

City _____ State_____ Zip _____

Web Site _____Telephone _____ *Include area code.*

Name(s) on Account _____

Type of Account _____ Account Number _____

Automatic Deposits _____

Automatic Drafts _____

Safe Deposit Box Number _____ Debit Card Number _____

Always have at least two signers on your safe deposit box plus your executor. Keep documents that are difficult or expensive to replace in the box. Keep copies of the documents at home.

Financial Institution _____ *Person A*

Address _____

City _____ State _____ Zip _____

Web Site _____Telephone _____ *Include area code.*

Name(s) on Account _____

Type of Account _____ Account Number _____

Automatic Deposits from_____

Automatic Drafts by_____

Financial Institution _____ *Person A*

Address _____

City _____ State _____ Zip _____

Web Site _____Telephone _____ *Include area code.*

Name(s) on Account _____

Type of Account _____ Account Number _____

Automatic Deposits from_____

Automatic Drafts by_____

Credit Cards

Financial Institution _____ *Person A*

Address _____

City _____ State _____ Zip _____

Web Site _____Telephone _____ *Include area code.*

Name(s) on Account _____

Account Number _____

Automatic Charges _____

_____

Financial Institution _____ *Person A*

Address _____

City _____ State _____ Zip _____

Web Site _____Telephone _____ *Include area code.*

Name(s) on Account _____

Account Number _____

Automatic Charges _____

_____

Financial Institution _____ *Person A*

Address _____

City _____ State _____ Zip _____

Web Site _____Telephone _____ *Include area code.*

Name(s) on Account _____

Account Number _____

Automatic Charges _____

_____

Check your credit report at least once a year to see if there is any unusual activity or errors. You are entitled to one free report a year from each of the credit agencies. To get the free reports, you must go through this web site: annualcreditreport.com.

Credit Cards

Financial Institution _____ *Person A*

Address _____

City _____ State _____ Zip _____

Web Site _____Telephone _____ *Include area code.*

Name(s) on Account _____

Account Number _____

Automatic Charges _____

_____

Financial Institution _____ *Person A*

Address _____

City _____ State _____ Zip _____

Web Site _____Telephone _____ *Include area code.*

Name(s) on Account _____

Account Number _____

Automatic Charges _____

_____

Financial Institution _____ *Person A*

Address _____

City _____ State _____ Zip _____

Web Site _____Telephone _____ *Include area code.*

Name(s) on Account _____

Account Number _____

Automatic Charges _____

_____

Check your credit report at least once a year to see if there is any unusual activity or errors. You are entitled to one free report a year from each of the credit agencies. To get the free reports, you must go through this web site: annualcreditreport.com.

Debts Owed

Debt owed <u>by</u> Person A *Example: installment contract for furniture or appliance*

Company _____

Telephone _____ *Include area code.*

How paid _____ *check or automatic withdrawal*

Frequency of payment _____ *monthly, quarterly, yearly*

Debt owed <u>by</u> Person A *Example: home equity loan*

Company _____

Telephone _____ *Include area code.*

How paid _____ *check or automatic withdrawal*

Frequency of payment _____ *monthly, quarterly, yearly*

Loans co-signed by Person A *List names of cosigners and creditors*

_____

_____

Mortgage for Primary Residence

Financial Institution _____ *Person A*

Address _____

City _____ State _____ Zip _____

Web Site _____ Telephone _____ *Include area code.*

Account Number _____

Property Taxes Paid with Mortgage? ☐ Yes ☐ No

Home Insurance Paid with Mortgage? ☐ Yes ☐ No

Mortgage for Secondary Residence

Financial Institution _____ *Person A*

Address _____

City _____ State _____ Zip _____

Web Site _____ Telephone _____ *Include area code.*

Account Number _____

Property Taxes Paid with Mortgage? ☐ Yes ☐ No

Home Insurance Paid with Mortgage? ☐ Yes ☐ No

On the Record/ Advance Planning

Sources of Income

Employment

Employer _____ *Person A*

Address _____

City _____ State _____ Zip _____

Web Site _____

Human Resources Department Telephone _____ *Include area code.*

Call for information on life insurance, medical insurance, COBRA and any information for income tax records.

Alimony/Child Support/Trust

Payer _____

Address _____

City _____ State _____ Zip _____

Telephone _____ *Include area code.*

How paid _____ *check or automatic deposit*

Frequency of payment _____ *monthly, quarterly, yearly*

Rent/Royalty/Oil & Gas Leases

Company _____

Telephone _____ *Include area code.*

How paid _____ *check or automatic deposit*

Frequency of payment _____ *monthly, quarterly, yearly*

Debt Owed to Person A

Payer _____

Telephone _____ *Include area code.*

How paid _____ *check or automatic deposit*

Frequency of payment _____ *monthly, quarterly, yearly*

Disposition at death _____ *estate, forgiven, bequest*

Investment Accounts *Include online brokerage accounts*

Financial Institution _____ *Person A*

Address _____

City _____ State _____ Zip _____

Telephone _____ *Include area code.*

Web Site _____

Name(s) on Account _____

Account Number _____

Financial Institution _____ *Person A*

Address _____

City _____ State _____ Zip _____

Telephone _____ *Include area code.*

Web Site _____

Name(s) on Account _____

Account Number _____

Bonds *List titled names, amounts and serial numbers and location*

_____

_____

_____

_____

Stock certificates *List company, titled names, certificate numbers, and location*

_____

_____

_____

_____

Consider filing stock certificates with a broker who will keep a "book record." Replacing or re-titling stock certificates in instances of loss, destruction, or inheritance is very expensive and time-consuming.

On the Record Advance Planning™

Special Custodial Accounts *Example: 529 for college education*

Financial Institution _____

Address _____

City _____ State _____ Zip _____

Telephone _____ *Include area code.*

Web Site _____

Name(s) on Account _____

Account Number _____

Financial Institution _____

Address _____

City _____ State _____ Zip _____

Telephone _____ *Include area code.*

Web Site _____

Name(s) on Account _____

Account Number _____

Financial Institution _____

Address _____

City _____ State _____ Zip _____

Telephone _____ *Include area code.*

Web Site _____

Name(s) on Account _____

Account Number _____

Retirement Accounts

Financial Institution _____

Address _____

City _____ State _____ Zip _____

Telephone _____ *Include area code.*

Web Site _____

Name on Account _____ *Person A*

Account Number _____

Type of Account _____ *Examples: IRA, Roth, 401(k), Keogh, SEP*

Primary Beneficiary _____

Secondary Beneficiary _____

Copy of Beneficiary forms filed _____ *location*

Financial Institution _____

Address _____

City _____ State _____ Zip _____

Telephone _____ *Include area code.*

Web Site _____

Name on Account _____ *Person A*

Account Number _____

Type of Account _____ *Examples: IRA, Roth, 401(k), Keogh, SEP*

Primary Beneficiary _____

Secondary Beneficiary _____

Copy of Beneficiary forms filed _____ *location*

Verify that your beneficiary forms are current. Check your account online or call the 800# for your retirement plan administrator. If you need to complete the forms again, follow these steps. Get the blank form. Make a copy of the blank form. Complete the form and sign it. Make a copy of the completed form. Keep the copy and the blank form in your files. Send the form with the original signature to the retirement plan administrator. The next time you need to change your beneficiaries, you will have a spare form on file.

Pension Accounts

Employer _____ *Person A*

Plan Administrator _____

Address _____

City _____ State _____ Zip _____

Telephone _____ *Include area code.*

Web Site _____

Qualified Domestic Relations Order naming _____

Qualified Domestic Relations Order filed _____ *location*

Account Number _____

Beneficiary _____

Copy of Beneficiary forms filed _____ *location*

Employer _____ *Person A*

Plan Administrator _____

Address _____

City _____ State _____ Zip _____

Telephone _____ *Include area code.*

Web Site _____

Qualified Domestic Relations Order naming _____

Qualified Domestic Relations Order filed _____ *location*

Account Number _____

Beneficiary _____

Copy of Beneficiary forms filed _____ *location*

Verify that your beneficiary forms are current. Check your account online or call the 800# for your pension plan administrator. If you need to complete the forms again, follow these steps. Get the blank form. Make a copy of the blank form. Complete the form and sign it. Make a copy of the completed form. Keep the copy and the blank form in your files. Send the form with the original signature to the pension plan administrator. The next time you need to change your beneficiaries, you will have a spare form on file.

Life Insurance Policies

Company _____

Address _____

City _____ State _____ Zip _____

Telephone _____ *Include area code.*

Web Site _____

Policy Number _____

Type of Policy _____ *Examples: whole, term*

Face Value of Policy _____ *optional*

Name of Insured _____ *Person A*

Primary Beneficiary _____

Secondary Beneficiary _____

Copy of Beneficiary forms filed _____ *location*

Company _____

Address _____

City _____ State _____ Zip _____

Telephone _____ *Include area code.*

Web Site _____

Policy Number _____

Type of Policy _____ *Examples: whole, term*

Face Value of Policy _____ *optional*

Name of Insured _____ *Person A*

Primary Beneficiary _____

Secondary Beneficiary _____

Copy of Beneficiary forms filed _____ *location*

Verify that your beneficiary forms are current. Check your account online or call the 800# for your insurance company. If you need to complete the forms again, follow these steps. Get the blank form. Make a copy. Complete the form and sign it. Make a copy of the completed form. Keep the copy and the blank form in your files. Send the form with the original signature to the insurance company. The next time you need to change your beneficiaries, you will have a spare form on file.

Statements for Financial Accounts

Paper filed _____

Electronic filed _____

Back-up stored _____

Remember that the best back-up is stored in another location such as your safe deposit box.

Professional Contacts

CPA/Tax Preparer _____

Address _____

City _____ State _____ Zip _____

Web Site _____

E-mail _____

Telephone _____ *Include area code.*

Financial Advisor _____

Address _____

City _____ State _____ Zip _____

Web Site _____

E-mail _____

Telephone _____ *Include area code.*

Banking

Financial Institution _____ *Person B*

Address _____

City _____ State _____ Zip _____

Web Site _____Telephone _____ *Include area code.*

Name(s) on Account _____

Type of Account _____ Account Number _____

Automatic Deposits _____

Automatic Drafts _____

Safe Deposit Box Number _____ Debit Card Number _____

Always have at least two signers on your safe deposit box plus your executor. Keep documents that are difficult or expensive to replace in the box. Keep copies of the documents at home.

Financial Institution _____ *Person B*

Address _____

City _____ State _____ Zip _____

Web Site _____Telephone _____ *Include area code.*

Name(s) on Account _____

Type of Account _____ Account Number _____

Automatic Deposits from_____

Automatic Drafts by_____

Financial Institution _____ *Person B*

Address _____

City _____ State _____ Zip _____

Web Site _____Telephone _____ *Include area code.*

Name(s) on Account _____

Type of Account _____ Account Number _____

Automatic Deposits from_____

Automatic Drafts by_____

On the Record Advance Planning

Credit Cards

Financial Institution _____ *Person B*

Address _____

City _____ State _____ Zip _____

Web Site _____Telephone _____ *Include area code.*

Name(s) on Account _____

Account Number _____

Automatic Charges _____

_____

Financial Institution _____ *Person B*

Address _____

City _____ State _____ Zip _____

Web Site _____Telephone _____ *Include area code.*

Name(s) on Account _____

Account Number _____

Automatic Charges _____

_____

Financial Institution _____ *Person B*

Address _____

City _____ State _____ Zip _____

Web Site _____Telephone _____ *Include area code.*

Name(s) on Account _____

Account Number _____

Automatic Charges _____

_____

Check your credit report at least once a year to see if there is any unusual activity or errors. You are entitled to one free report a year from each of the credit agencies. To get the free reports, you must go through this web site: annualcreditreport.com.

On the Record: Advance Planning

Credit Cards

Financial Institution _____ *Person B*

Address _____

City _____ State _____ Zip _____

Web Site _____Telephone _____ *Include area code.*

Name(s) on Account _____

Account Number _____

Automatic Charges _____

_____

Financial Institution _____ *Person B*

Address _____

City _____ State _____ Zip _____ *Include area code.*

Web Site _____Telephone _____

Name(s) on Account _____

Account Number _____

Automatic Charges _____

_____

Financial Institution _____ *Person B*

Address _____

City _____ State _____ Zip _____

Web Site _____Telephone _____ *Include area code.*

Name(s) on Account _____

Account Number _____

Automatic Charges _____

_____

Check your credit report at least once a year to see if there is any unusual activity or errors. You are entitled to one free report a year from each of the credit agencies. To get the free reports, you must go through this web site: annualcreditreport.com.

On the Record/Advance Planning™

Debts Owed

Debt owed <u>by</u> Person B *Example: installment contract for furniture or appliance*

Company _____

Telephone _____ *Include area code.*

How paid _____ *check or automatic withdrawal*

Frequency of payment _____ *monthly, quarterly, yearly*

Debt owed <u>by</u> Person B *Example: home equity loan*

Company _____

Telephone _____ *Include area code.*

How paid _____ *check or automatic withdrawal*

Frequency of payment _____ *monthly, quarterly, yearly*

Loans co-signed by Person B *List names of cosigners and creditors*

_____

_____

Mortgage for Primary Residence

Financial Institution _____ *Person B*

Address _____

City _____ State _____ Zip _____ *Include area code.*

Web Site _____ Telephone _____

Account Number _____

Property Taxes Paid with Mortgage? ☐ Yes ☐ No

Home Insurance Paid with Mortgage? ☐ Yes ☐ No

Mortgage for Secondary Residence

Financial Institution _____ *Person B*

Address _____

City _____ State _____ Zip _____ *Include area code.*

Web Site _____ Telephone _____

Account Number _____

Property Taxes Paid with Mortgage? ☐ Yes ☐ No

Home Insurance Paid with Mortgage? ☐ Yes ☐ No

Sources of Income

Employment

Employer _____ *Person B*

Address _____

City _____ State _____ Zip _____

Web Site _____

Human Resources Department Telephone _____ *Include area code.*

Call for information on life insurance, medical insurance, COBRA and any information for income tax records.

Alimony/Child Support/Trust

Payer _____

Address _____

City _____ State _____ Zip _____

Telephone _____ *Include area code.*

How paid _____ *check or automatic deposit*

Frequency of payment _____ *monthly, quarterly, yearly*

Rent/Royalty/Oil & Gas Leases

Company _____

Telephone _____ *Include area code.*

How paid _____ *check or automatic deposit*

Frequency of payment _____ *monthly, quarterly, yearly*

Debt Owed to Person B

Payer _____

Telephone _____ *Include area code.*

How paid _____ *check or automatic deposit*

Frequency of payment _____ *monthly, quarterly, yearly*

Disposition at death _____ *estate, forgiven, bequest*

Investment Accounts *Include online brokerage accounts*

Financial Institution _____ *Person B*

Address _____

City _____ State _____ Zip _____

Telephone _____ *Include area code.*

Web Site _____

Name(s) on Account _____

Account Number _____

Financial Institution _____ *Person B*

Address _____

City _____ State _____ Zip _____

Telephone _____ *Include area code.*

Web Site _____

Name(s) on Account _____

Account Number _____

Bonds *List titled names, amounts and serial numbers and location*

_____

_____

_____

_____

Stock certificates *List company, titled names, certificate numbers, and location*

_____

_____

_____

_____

Consider filing stock certificates with a broker who will keep a "book record." Replacing or re-titling stock certificates in instances of loss, destruction, or inheritance is very expensive and time-consuming.

Special Custodial Accounts *Example: 529 for college education*

Financial Institution _____

Address _____

City _____ State _____ Zip _____

Telephone _____ *Include area code.*

Web Site _____

Name(s) on Account _____

Account Number _____

Financial Institution _____

Address _____

City _____ State _____ Zip _____

Telephone _____ *Include area code.*

Web Site _____

Name(s) on Account _____

Account Number _____

Financial Institution _____

Address _____

City _____ State _____ Zip _____

Telephone _____ *Include area code.*

Web Site _____

Name(s) on Account _____

Account Number _____

Retirement Accounts

Financial Institution _____

Address _____

City _____ State _____ Zip _____

Telephone _____ *Include area code.*

Web Site _____

Name on Account _____ *Person B*

Account Number _____

Type of Account _____ *Examples: IRA, Roth, 401(k), Keogh, SEP*

Primary Beneficiary _____

Secondary Beneficiary _____

Copy of Beneficiary forms filed _____ *location*

Financial Institution _____

Address _____

City _____ State _____ Zip _____

Telephone _____ *Include area code.*

Web Site _____

Name on Account _____ *Person B*

Account Number _____

Type of Account _____ *Examples: IRA, Roth, 401(k), Keogh, SEP*

Primary Beneficiary _____

Secondary Beneficiary _____

Copy of Beneficiary forms filed _____ *location*

Verify that your beneficiary forms are current. Check your account online or call the 800# for your retirement plan administrator. If you need to complete the forms again, follow these steps. Get the blank form. Make a copy of the blank form. Complete the form and sign it. Make a copy of the completed form. Keep the copy and the blank form in your files. Send the form with the original signature to the retirement plan administrator. The next time you need to change your beneficiaries, you will have a spare form on file.

Pension Accounts

Employer _____ *Person B*

Plan Administrator _____

Address _____

City _____ State _____ Zip _____

Telephone _____ *Include area code.*

Web Site _____

Qualified Domestic Relations Order naming _____

Qualified Domestic Relations Order filed _____ *location*

Account Number _____

Beneficiary _____

Copy of Beneficiary forms filed _____ *location*

Employer _____ *Person B*

Plan Administrator _____

Address _____

City _____ State _____ Zip _____

Telephone _____ *Include area code.*

Web Site _____

Qualified Domestic Relations Order naming _____

Qualified Domestic Relations Order filed _____ *location*

Account Number _____

Beneficiary _____

Copy of Beneficiary forms filed _____ *location*

Verify that your beneficiary forms are current. Check your account online or call the 800# for your pension plan administrator. If you need to complete the forms again, follow these steps. Get the blank form. Make a copy of the blank form. Complete the form and sign it. Make a copy of the completed form. Keep the copy and the blank form in your files. Send the form with the original signature to the pension plan administrator. The next time you need to change your beneficiaries, you will have a spare form on file.

Life Insurance Policies

Company _____

Address _____

City _____ State _____ Zip _____

Telephone _____ *Include area code.*

Web Site _____

Policy Number _____

Type of Policy _____ *Examples: whole, term*

Face Value of Policy _____ *optional*

Name of Insured _____ *Person B*

Primary Beneficiary _____

Secondary Beneficiary _____

Copy of Beneficiary forms filed _____ *location*

Company _____

Address _____

City _____ State _____ Zip _____

Telephone _____ *Include area code.*

Web Site _____

Policy Number _____

Type of Policy _____ *Examples: whole, term*

Face Value of Policy _____ *optional*

Name of Insured _____ *Person B*

Primary Beneficiary _____

Secondary Beneficiary _____

Copy of Beneficiary forms filed _____ *location*

Verify that your beneficiary forms are current. Check your online or call the 800# for your insurance company. If you need to complete the forms again, follow these steps. Get the blank form. Make a copy. Complete the form and sign it. Make a copy of the completed form. Keep the copy and the blank form in your files. Send the form with the original signature to the insurance company. The next time you need to change your beneficiaries, you will have a spare form on file.

Statements for Financial Accounts

Paper filed _____

Electronic filed _____

Back-up stored _____

Remember that the best back-up is stored in another location such as your safe deposit box.

Professional Contacts

CPA/Tax Preparer _____

Address _____

City _____ State _____ Zip _____

Web Site _____

E-mail _____

Telephone _____ *Include area code.*

Financial Advisor _____

Address _____

City _____ State _____ Zip _____

Web Site _____

E-mail _____

Telephone _____ *Include area code.*

On the Record/Advance Planning™

Personal Property

"A place for everything and everything in its place."
Isabella Mary Beeton, *The Book of Household Management,* 1861

Background

Information about a mortgage is repeated here so you need only to look up the information in the Financial Information section.

Tasks

- ❑ Complete Personal Property section for your household.
- ❑ Store your deed and title insurance papers in a safe deposit box.
- ❑ Inventory your valuable such as jewelry, antiques, and fire arms. Put copy of inventory in safe deposit box.
- ❑ Make back-up copies of your photographs. Store negatives or electronic copies in a safe deposit box or store electronic copies with an online back-up service.
- ❑ Store automobile titles in a safe deposit box.

Resource

Who Gets Grandma's Yellow Pie Plate?
Order workbook, video, or educator's package from:
University of Minnesota Extension Service Distribution Center
405 Coffey Hall, 1420 Eckles Av
St. Paul, MN 55108
800-876-8636
http://shop.extension.umn.edu/SearchResults.aspx?KeyWords=grandma&searchType=Store

Bonus Ideas

Shop for homeowner's or renter's and automobile insurance periodically. You can research insurance rates online or work with an independent insurance agent who can compare rates across companies. It is helpful to have photographs of special items such as jewelry or antiques or fire arms. Store photographs or negatives in a safe place.

Consider whether you really need to pay for a storage unit.

Leave a written expression of your wishes for the disposition of your tangible personal possessions. Many persons who leave a will nonetheless neglect to provide clear instructions regarding who is to inherit what personal items or family heirlooms.

You will add meaning to your gifts of personal items and family heirlooms if you tell why an item is meaningful to you and share stories about family members.

Primary Residence

Address_____

City _____ State _____ Zip _____

Mortgage Company/Owner _____

Address _____

City _____ State _____ Zip _____

Web Site _____

Telephone _____ *Include area code.*

Account Number _____

Property Deed filed _____ *location*

Property Taxes Paid with Mortgage?   ☐ Yes ☐ No

    If no, county where taxes are paid _____

Home Insurance Paid with Mortgage?   ☐ Yes ☐ No

Secondary Residence

Address_____

City _____ State _____ Zip _____

Mortgage Company/Owner _____

Address _____

City _____ State _____ Zip _____

Web Site _____

Telephone _____ *Include area code.*

Account Number _____

Property Deed filed_____ *location*

Property Taxes Paid with Mortgage?   ☐ Yes ☐ No

    If no, county where taxes are paid _____

Home Insurance Paid with Mortgage?   ☐ Yes ☐ No

Home Insurance

Insurance Agent _____

Company Name _____

Address _____

City _____ State _____ Zip _____

Web site _____

Telephone _____ *Include area code.*

E-mail address _____

Policy Number _____

Storage Unit

Address _____

City _____ State _____ Zip _____

Storage Company _____

Unit Number _____ Keys/Combination _____

Payment Due Date _____ *Examples: 20th of month or every July 1st*

Photographs & Back-ups

You may want to note where you store negatives or the electronic versions of your treasured photographs.

Remember that a good back-up is stored in another location such as a safe deposit box or a relative's home.

Valuables

You may want to make a list of valuable jewelry or antiques even if you do not have a separate insurance rider. Include fire arms and ammunition on this list as well.

Automobiles

Make _____ Model _____ Year _____

VIN _____ Registration Expires _____ *month*

Owned? If yes, title filed _____ *location*

If no, Lessor or Lien Holder _____

Address _____

City _____ State _____ Zip _____

Telephone _____ *Include area code.*

Account Number _____

Make _____ Model _____ Year _____

VIN _____ Registration Expires _____ *month*

Owned? If yes, title filed _____ *location*

If no, Lessor or Lien Holder _____

Address _____

City _____ State _____ Zip _____

Telephone _____ *Include area code.*

Account Number _____

Make _____ Model _____ Year _____

VIN _____ Registration Expires _____ *month*

Owned? If yes, title filed _____ *location*

If no, Lessor or Lien Holder _____

Address _____

City _____ State _____ Zip _____

Telephone _____ *Include area code.*

Account Number _____

Recreational Vehicle or Other Vehicle or Boat

Make _____Model _____ Year _____

VIN _____ Registration Expires _____ *month*

Owned? If yes, title filed _____ *location*

If no, Lessor or Lien Holder _____

Address _____

City _____ State _____ Zip _____

Telephone _____ *Include area code.*

Account Number _____

Recreational Vehicle or Other Vehicle or Boat Storage

Address _____

City _____ State _____ Zip _____

Telephone _____ *Include area code.*

Lessor _____

Slip or Lot Number _____ Keys/Combination _____

Payment Due Date _____ *Examples: 20th of month or every July 1st*

Automobile & Other Vehicle & Boat Insurance

Insurance Agent _____

Company Name _____

Address _____

City _____ State _____ Zip _____

Web Site _____

Telephone _____ *Include area code.*

E-mail address _____

Policy Number _____

Household Facts

"Getting your house in order and reducing the confusion gives you more control over your life. Personal organization somehow releases or frees you to operate more effectively."
Larry King

Background

You may not need to use all entries. Think of this section as information a house sitter would need if you went on vacation for a month.

You can enter information on:
- Utilities
- Household services
- Pets and livestock
- Persons who have keys

and notes on:
- Seasonal maintenance
- Repair services
- File location for manuals and warranties
- Location of home safe.

Tasks

- ❑ Complete Household Facts section for your household.
- ❑ Shred old utility statements.
- ❑ Discard manuals for appliances you no longer own and warranties that have expired.

Resources

Refer to utility or service company statements for information to record. If you decide you want to know your water or electric usage pattern, you can often get this information online from your utility.

Bonus Ideas

You can shred an old statement when you receive the next one showing that payment was received unless you have a home office and need the documentation for your tax return. If you shred as you go, you will not accumulate files or piles of paper to review later.

Oil your shredder at least once a month to prevent burning up your machine.

Utilities

Water Company _____

Address _____

City _____ State _____ Zip _____

Telephone _____ *Include area code.*

Account Number _____

Electric Company _____

Address _____

City _____ State _____ Zip _____

Telephone _____ *Include area code.*

Account Number _____

Gas Company _____

Address _____

City _____ State _____ Zip _____

Telephone _____ *Include area code.*

Account Number _____

Trash Removal Company _____

Address _____

City _____ State _____ Zip _____

Telephone _____ *Include area code.*

Account Number _____

Day of Week for Trash Pickup _____

Day of Week for Recycling Pickup _____

Think of this section as information a house sitter would need if you went on vacation for a month.

Utilities, continued

Telephone Company _____

For telephone number_____☐ Home ☐ Office ☐ Cell

Address _____ *Include area code.*

City _____ State _____ Zip _____

Telephone _____ *Include area code.*

Account Number _____

Telephone Company _____

For telephone number_____☐ Home ☐ Office ☐ Cell

Address _____ *Include area code.*

City _____ State _____ Zip _____

Telephone _____ *Include area code.*

Account Number _____

Telephone Company _____

For telephone number_____☐ Home ☐ Office ☐ Cell

Address _____ *Include area code.*

City _____ State _____ Zip _____

Telephone _____ *Include area code.*

Account Number _____

Internet Service Provider _____

Address _____

City _____ State _____ Zip _____

Telephone _____ *Include area code.*

Account Number _____

Note if internet service provider is the same as telephone and/or television service provider.

Utilities, continued

Television Company _____ *cable or satellite*

Address _____

City _____ State _____ Zip _____

Telephone _____ *Include area code.*

Account Number _____

Yard Service _____

Address _____

City _____ State _____ Zip _____

Telephone _____ *Include area code.*

Account Number _____

Cleaning Service _____

Address _____

City _____ State _____ Zip _____

Telephone _____ *Include area code.*

Account Number _____

Alarm Company _____

Address _____

City _____ State _____ Zip _____

Telephone _____ *Include area code.*

Account Number _____

Location of key pad for alarm system _____ *Example: by front door*

Location of codes for alarm system _____ *Example: user's manual*

Utilities, continued

Other Service _____ *Example: pest control*

Address _____

City _____ State _____ Zip _____

Telephone _____ *Include area code.*

Account Number _____

Other Service _____ *Example: pool service*

Address _____

City _____ State _____ Zip _____

Telephone _____ *Include area code.*

Account Number _____

Other Service _____ *Example: lawn treatment*

Address _____

City _____ State _____ Zip _____

Telephone _____ *Include area code.*

Account Number _____

Other Service _____ *Example: HOA*

Address _____

City _____ State _____ Zip _____

Telephone _____ *Include area code.*

Account Number _____

Current billed filed _____ *location*

Electronic bills received at _____ *e-mail address*

Electronic bills debited at _____ *bank account*

Pets

Name and Type of Pet _____

_____

Examples: Puddles the dog, Cuddles the cat; Fluffy the goldfish

Veterinarian _____

Address _____

City _____ State _____ Zip _____

Telephone _____ *Include area code.*

E-mail address _____

Name and Type of Pet _____

_____

Examples: Puddles the dog, Cuddles the cat; Fluffy the goldfish

Veterinarian _____

Address _____

City _____ State _____ Zip _____

Telephone _____ *Include area code.*

E-mail address _____

Persons Who Have Extra Keys

Name _____

Address _____

City _____ State _____ Zip _____

Telephone _____ *Include area code.*

Name _____

Address _____

City _____ State _____ Zip _____

Telephone _____ *Include area code.*

On the Record/Advance Planning

Seasonal Maintenance & Repair Services

System	Month(s)	Service Provider	Telephone
Example: HVAC	*Apr. & Oct.*	*Johnson Brothers Heating & Air*	*Include area code.*
_____	_____	_____	_____
_____	_____	_____	_____
_____	_____	_____	_____
_____	_____	_____	_____
_____	_____	_____	_____
_____	_____	_____	_____
_____	_____	_____	_____
_____	_____	_____	_____
_____	_____	_____	_____
_____	_____	_____	_____
_____	_____	_____	_____
_____	_____	_____	_____

Manuals and Warranties filed _____ *location*

Take a moment to sort through your file of manuals and warranties. Discard manuals for appliances you no longer own and warranties that have expired.

Home Safe or Fireproof Box

Location _____ *Example: bedroom closet*

Person with combination _____

Telephone _____ *Include area code.*

Document Locator

"Good order is the foundation of all things."
Edmund Burke

Background

You probably file your documents in a few different places. Designate one, perhaps the safe deposit box, as Location A. Enter in "safe deposit box" next to Location A. Check column A for all the documents stored in the safe deposit box. Follow the same procedure for Location B which might be the desk drawer and Location C which might be the file cabinet in the office closet.

If you store documents in more than three locations, consider simplifying your system. Simplifying your system may include consolidating files in one location, purging outdated files, or both.

If you store original documents in the safe deposit box, consider keeping copies at home so that the information is readily available.

Task

❑   Complete Document Locator section for your household.

Resource

Refer to already completed sections of your workbook.

Bonus Idea

You may find your completed workbook a handy reference for yourself.

Location A _____   *Example: safe deposit box*

Location B _____   *Example: file cabinet*

Location C _____   *Example: hall closet*

	A	**B**	**C**
Personal Papers			
Birth Certificate	_____	_____	_____
Marriage Certificate	_____	_____	_____
Divorce Decree	_____	_____	_____
Death Certificate	_____	_____	_____
Social Security Card	_____	_____	_____
Passport _____ *Number*	_____	_____	_____
Military Discharge Papers (DD214)	_____	_____	_____
Other _____	_____	_____	_____

Examples: Adoption or Citizenship papers

	A	**B**	**C**
Medical Directives			
Directive Regarding Who May Receive Information	_____	_____	_____
Advance Directive to Doctor & Family/Surrogates	_____	_____	_____
Medical Power of Attorney	_____	_____	_____
Organ Card or Body Donation Forms	_____	_____	_____
Out of Hospital Do Not Resuscitate Order	_____	_____	_____

	A	**B**	**C**
Last Rituals			
Pre-paid Funeral Contract	_____	_____	_____
Pre-paid Cemetery Plot or Columbarium Contract	_____	_____	_____
Instructions for Funeral or Memorial Service	_____	_____	_____

	A	B	C

Legal Documents

	A	B	C
Will	_____	_____	_____
Durable Power of Attorney	_____	_____	_____
Trust	_____	_____	_____
Key Document _____	_____	_____	_____
Key Document _____	_____	_____	_____
Key Document _____	_____	_____	_____

Examples: Divorce decree or Pre-Nuptial agreement

Financial Documents

	A	B	C
Medical Insurance Policies	_____	_____	_____
Life Insurance Policies	_____	_____	_____
Current Bills	_____	_____	_____
Tax Returns (recent)	_____	_____	_____
Tax Returns (back years)	_____	_____	_____
Other _____	_____	_____	_____

Example: Qualified Domestic Relations Order

Property Titles & Deeds

	A	B	C
Property Deeds	_____	_____	_____
Home Insurance Policy	_____	_____	_____
Cemetery Property Deed	_____	_____	_____
Storage Facility Contract	_____	_____	_____
Automobile & Other Vehicle Titles	_____	_____	_____
Automobile & Other Vehicle Insurance Policies	_____	_____	_____
Other _____	_____	_____	_____

Example: car leasing agreement

Professional Contacts

"A professional is someone who can do his best work when he doesn't feel like it."
Alistair Cooke

Background

The good news is that you have already gathered this information and need only to re-record it here. Remember that someone else is likely to use your workbook in an emergency. The information is repeated here so it is easy for someone else to find it quickly.

Task

❑ Complete Professional Contacts section for your household.

Resource

Refer to already completed sections of your workbook.

Bonus Idea

Celebrate completion of your critical information workbook!

Attorney _____

Address _____

City _____ State _____ Zip _____

E-mail _____

Telephone _____ *Include area code.*

Clergy/Spiritual Advisor _____

Address _____

City _____ State _____ Zip _____

E-mail _____

Telephone _____ *Include area code.*

CPA/Tax Preparer _____

Address _____

City _____ State _____ Zip _____

E-mail _____

Telephone _____ *Include area code.*

Dentist _____ for _____ *Person A*

Address _____

City _____ State _____ Zip _____

E-mail _____

Telephone _____ *Include area code.*

Dentist _____ for _____ *Person B*

Address _____

City _____ State _____ Zip _____

E-mail _____

Telephone _____ *Include area code.*

On the Record/ Advance Planning

*Doctor (Primary Care)*_____ for _____ *Person A*

Address _____

City _____State_____ Zip_____

E-mail _____

Telephone _____ *Include area code.*

Doctor(Primary Care) _____ for _____ *Person B*

Address _____

City _____State_____ Zip_____

E-mail _____

Telephone _____ *Include area code.*

Employer _____ for _____ *Person A*

Address _____

City _____ State_____ Zip _____

Human Resources Contact _____

Telephone _____ *Include area code.*

Employer _____ for _____ *Person B*

Address _____

City _____ State_____ Zip _____

Human Resources Contact _____

Telephone _____ *Include area code.*

Financial Advisor _____

Address _____

City _____State_____ Zip_____

E-mail _____

Telephone _____ *Include area code.*

Insurance Agent _____

Address _____

City _____State_____ Zip_____

E-mail _____

Telephone _____ *Include area code.*

Pharmacist _____

Address _____

City _____State_____ Zip_____

Telephone _____ *Include area code.*

Acknowledgements

This work book was not developed overnight by a single person. It has evolved over time. A number of people have reviewed drafts and made suggestions about clarity and content. I would like to thank: Bobbie Allar, Kelly Burns, Jim Cooper, Jody and Jerry Cooke, Lydia Deats, Mary Anne Doyle, Olga Garza, Rob Gearhart, Jeanne Guy, Jeff and Gale Hamilton, Tommie Huggins, Joyce Inman, Julie Kennedy, Mary Koffend, Louis Kokernak, Al and Jan Kuebler, Mike McCloskey, Meg O'Brien, Johnnie Overton, Laurie and Kelly Parkhill, Richard and Toi Powell, Heidi Spock, Brenda Staples, Susan Taylor, Nancy Walker, and Debbie and John Warden.

You, too, are welcome to write with your comments and suggestions.
Visit www.OnTheRecordOrganizing.com/contact-us to comment.

About the Author

Amy Praskac reunited with her high school sweetheart only to be widowed a few years later. Her experience served as a springboard for a new career as a professional organizer specializing in end-of-life planning. She blogs at *Amy on Organizing Records*.

Learn more about Amy Praskac and *On the Record Advance Planning* at www.OnTheRecordOrganizing.com.

Made in the USA
Monee, IL
02 November 2020